Design and illustration by Cricket Design Works, Madison, WI

Self-published in the United States by Beginner's Mind™

ISBN 978-0-692-81107-8

Copyright © 2016 Beginner's Mind LLC. All Rights Reserved.

For ordering information, please see our website:

beginnersmindresources.com

CONTENTS

What Is Beginners Mind?   2
What is Mindfulness and Why Is it Good for Your Child?   4
Why I Created This Home Kit   6
How to Use This Book   8

Getting Started   13
1. What Is Mindfulness?   14
2. Read-Aloud   16
3. Clear Mind Jar   16
4. Tuning In to Sound   20
5. Gratitude Chains   22

Mindful Breathing Activities   26
A Few Tips Before Practicing Breathing Activities   28
1. Breathing In, Breathing Out: 1   30
2. Body Scan   32
3. Four-Corner Breath   34
4. High Five   36
5. Filling the Balloon   37
6. What Type Are You?   38
7. Belly Breathing: Sitting   39
8. Heart Breath   40

9. Buzzing Like a Bee	41
10. Robot Hands	42
11. Breathing In, Breathing Out: 2	42
12. Calming Breath	43
13. Noticing What You Notice	44
14. Belly Breathing: Lying Down	45
15. Practicing Breath Control	46
Affirmations	47
Mudras for Children	48

Exploring the Five Senses   50

Smell   52
1. Mindful Walk	54
2. No-Sew Eye Pillows With or Without Essential Oils	55
3. What's that Smell?	57

Touch   58
1. Partner Drawing	60
2. Texture Rubbings	61
3. The Beauty of the Heartbeat	62
4. Mystery Boxes	63

Hearing 64
1. Tuning In to What's Around Us: Indoors 66
2. Tuning In to What's Around Us: Outdoors 67
3. Musical Mandala 68
4. Musical Drawing 69

Sight 70
1. What Do You Remember? 72
2. Mindful Walk 73
3. Rainbow Walk 74
4. Cloud Watch 75

Taste 76
1. Timed Meal 78
2. Blindfolded Taste Test 79
3. Mindful Tasting Using the Other Senses 79
4. Exploring All Five Senses 80

Gratitude 82
1. Pass the Gratitude 84
2. Gratitude Journals 84
3. Gratitude Jar 85

Kindness — 86

1. Kindness Hearts — 88
2. Thinking Kind Acts — 89
3. Peace Flags — 91
4. Kindness Bingo — 92
5. Acts of Kindness — 94

Empathy — 96

Things to Keep in Mind When Teaching Empathy — 98
1. Nature Walk — 99
2. Stand in My Shoes — 100
3. Toothpaste Challenge — 102
4. Family or Friend in Need — 103
5. Role Playing and Discussion — 104

Togetherness — 106

1. Circle Sit — 108
2. Pair/Group Sit — 109
3. Time at the Park or Playground — 109
4. Treasure Hunt — 110
5. Togetherness Time — 111

What Is Beginner's Mind?

A beginner's mind is one that is open and free of preconceived ideas, opinions and judgments. When we are born, we enter the world with a beginner's mind. Everything is new and all of our firsts are celebrated. As we grow, our minds become full of preconceived opinions and ideas. We want to show off our strengths and cover up our struggles. We reconnect with that beginner's mind through the practice of mindfulness. Through mindfulness, we are able to know and accept

that struggle is actually a part of learning. Once we let go of thinking we are experts, and keep our minds and hearts open, we can find that even a beginner has something to teach us.

When we see the world through the perspective of beginner's mind, each day is a new day and each moment is a new moment. We can appreciate who we are and what we have. We are able to be more kind, more compassionate and more empathetic toward others, and we end up living our lives in a more open and balanced way.

What is Mindfulness and Why Is it Good for Your Child?

Mindfulness is simply being aware of what is happening right now without wishing it were different; enjoying the pleasant without holding on when it changes (which it will); being with the unpleasant without fearing it will always be this way (which it won't).

— James Baraz

The purpose of being mindful is to find peace in everyday moments. Mindfulness is the practice of taking the time to fully experience what you notice about the present moment, and not dwelling on the past or focusing on the future. Our minds are constantly thinking, and at times it seems as though we don't have much control over what happens inside our own heads. But in a mindful state, we remain calmer and we are able to acknowledge thoughts and feelings without judging them — or ourselves — harshly. Mindfulness is the practice of being in control of your mind, rather than your mind controlling you.

Research has shown that practicing mindfulness also:

- improves self-control and reduces impulsive behaviors
- increases attention span
- improves academic performance
- increases awareness of the physical world around us
- helps us make peace with personal imperfections by teaching acceptance
- help us embrace vulnerability by learning to trust ourselves and others
- provides the avenue to be more gracious, empathetic, compassionate and kind to ourselves and others

Our brain is in charge of everything we do. Its many parts work together to cause us to think and feel, to move the way we move, and do the things we do. Mindfulness practice can literally change the way the brain works. Here's how: When we are anxious, overly excited, or in a very stressful situation, a bundle of neurons located in the center of the brain, called the amygdala (uh-MIG-duh-luh), sends messages to other parts of the brain. These messages help prepare the body to fight, flee, or freeze in response to threatening situations. When we are in this highly stressed state, our brains are very narrowly focused on reacting to whatever threat we perceive. We have a much harder time seeing the big picture, or making wise choices. Practicing mindful activities, such as breath work, recognizing and labeling our emotions, and connecting with ourselves, has been shown to shrink the amygdala, which in turn allows us to stay calmer and more able to send signals to the prefrontal cortex, the area of brain that makes rational decision-making and problem-solving possible. Mindfulness helps us to recognize that split-second between when something happens to us and when we respond to it, so that we can choose to act in wiser ways.

Why I Created This Home Kit

I am very grateful to have had the opportunity to work with young children in grades pre-K through five for more than 20 years. I started my career in education working with preschool children, both as a teacher and program coordinator. I then transitioned to the public school system and taught grades one to three, both in a multi-age and straight grade capacity. After obtaining a master's degree in education, I turned my focus toward instilling the love of reading and math in young children, and became a math and reading resource specialist and learning strategist.

Several years ago, I enrolled in a yoga teacher training program and became a yoga instructor (RYT 200). I wanted to delve deeper into my personal yoga practice, and to explore the reason behind why I felt so alive, yet so at peace after spending time on my mat. My yoga practice and training took me on the path of living a more mindful life. I soon realized that the more I practiced mindfulness, the more at peace I became with myself and the world around me.

I found that I was less anxious and less judgmental, and began to see life through a much clearer lens.

I wanted others to experience what I had found, and was eager to bring yoga and mindfulness practice into the schools. I began to teach yoga to other educators, and mindfulness lessons to students in school and community settings. In teaching mindfulness to children, I knew that I had found my passion.

I discovered that teachers like me were in need of an easy to use mindfulness program with all supplies included to teach elementary students in schools and community organizations. In June of 2016, The Beginner's Mind Mindfulness Teaching Toolkit was launched. Soon after, I had many requests from parents to develop an at-home toolkit for families and caregivers to bring mindfulness into homes on a smaller scale. This home kit is the answer to that request.

I thank you for purchasing the Beginner's Mind Mindfulness at Home kit and wish you the best on your journey of bringing the practice of mindfulness into your child's life.

Laura Zimmer, MA, RYT 200

How To Use This Book

This book was designed to teach children and their families the tools needed to live a more mindful life. Although it's intended for children ages 5-10, many of the activities can be modified for use with younger or older children as their caregivers see fit. You will notice as you move through the book that the activities refer to "your child." Please note that these activities can be done with more than one child or family member and if indicated, a larger group of people. Since children learn by example, practice these activities with your child and be mindful throughout your day to be more caring, compassionate and loving towards yourself and others. When you outwardly project a sense of calm and peace, your child will notice and follow in your footsteps.

In the elementary years, the best way for children to learn about the world around them is through direct experiences, modeling and active exploration. These activities offer children interactive, hands-on mindfulness experiences that help to bring peace into family life, foster community building, and provide children with an overall sense of well-being.

Materials

In this home kit, I have included a favorite book of mine that I like to share when I work with children, a percussion chime to signal breath work and quiet sitting, the supplies needed to make a clear mind jar, and a mandala coloring book to use as a way to de-stress and calm your child's ever-thinking mind.

You will notice that in the margin next to each activity is a list of other suggested materials. On the next page is a consolidated list of all materials you will need when using this book. Also included is a recommended book list. These are not required, but are nice to have to introduce some of the key concepts of mindfulness. Taking a trip to the library with your child to gather these titles provides a great opportunity to spend quality time together and help get her excited about beginning her mindfulness journey. If you are able to obtain the books before beginning the activities, read a book or two from the category you are introducing to your child. For example, a great book to introduce the concept of empathy before you begin that section is *Stand in My Shoes*, by Bob Sornson. Books also make great gifts, so adding some of these titles to your child's gift list is a great way to acquire these books.

Things to Gather Before You Begin

It is assumed that the following materials are either already in your home or easy to acquire by borrowing or purchasing. Feel free to modify any of the materials if you find you have something in your home that would work just as easily.

- Scissors
- Markers
- Crayons
- Pom-poms
- Straws
- Pinwheels
- Bubbles
- Colored paper
- White paper
- Tube sock
- Dry rice
- Blindfold or bandana

- 3-4 shoe boxes
- Small stuffed animal
- Journal
- Cardboard or tag board
- String or twine
- Athletic wrap or towel
- Calm music
- Hoberman Sphere
- Essential oils (optional)
- Various fun games, puzzles and books of your child's choice

Recommended Books

Mindfulness
What Does It Mean to Be Present? by Rana DiOrio (included)
Silence by Lemniscates
Take the Time by Maud Roegiers
The Lemonade Hurricane by Licia Morelli
Last Stop on Market Street by Matt de la Peña
Puppy Mind by Andrew Jordan Nance

Gratitude
Ordinary Mary's Extraordinary Deed by Emily Pearson
Gratitude Soup by Olivia Rosewood

Exploring the Five Senses
You Can't Taste a Pickle with your Ear by Harriet Ziefert
No Ordinary Apple by Sara Marlowe

Kindness
Ordinary Mary's Extraordinary Deed by Emily Pearson
The Invisible Boy by Trudy Ludwig
What Does It Mean to Be Kind? By Rana DiOrio

Empathy
Stand in My Shoes by Bob Sornson
Hey, Little Ant by Phillip and Hannah Hoose

Creating a Calm Space Within Your Home

Once you and your family have learned the tools needed to live a more mindful life, living mindfully can occur naturally in any setting and situation. However, creating a space within your home where family members can go when a warm, calming retreat is needed can provide added support for your family's mindfulness practice. If your space allows, find an area that is away from the whirlwind of life and make a peaceful sanctuary with your child. Ask him what is important for feeling calm and safe. Your family's calm space can make use of materials you already have in your home or it can be made into a more elaborate area depending on your space, finances and needs. Consider these items for inclusion in your calm space:

- large pillows or meditation cushions for quiet sitting
- lamps that provide soft lighting
- singing bowl or percussion chime for breath work
- soft music and headphones
- coloring books or mandalas with colored pencils
- journals or paper for finding peace in writing or drawing
- iPads with headphones for listening to soft music, guided meditations or visualizations
- puzzles or mazes to help redirect thoughts or anger
- Hoberman sphere to use as a guide through inhalations and exhalations
- kids' yoga books/cards with illustrated yoga poses for movement breaks
- tactile basket with stress balls, modeling clay, rollers, etc.
- blankets or pillows if getting cozy is what's needed

Getting Started

The following activities are a beautiful way to introduce mindfulness to children and lay the foundation for the subsequent activities in the Beginner's Mind Mindfulness At Home kit. I strongly encourage presenting these activities in the order provided before moving on.

GETTING STARTED

Activity 1: What is Mindfulness?

Begin this activity by sharing the "Are You Mind Full or Mindful?" picture on the next page with your child.

Give your child a few moments to sit quietly while she studies the picture. After a few moments, ask about what she sees in the picture. She may have noticed a dog and his owner out on a walk, or she may point out the busy cloud bubble above the boy's head and the not-so-busy cloud bubble above the dog. Feel free to discuss what you see to create conversation with your child.

Astute children may observe that the boy in the poster is missing out on what he is doing. His thought bubble is crowded with things that may have happened in the past or things that haven't happened yet. He is not taking notice of the fact that he is walking with his best friend on a beautiful, sunny day. **The boy's mind is full. The dog, on the other hand, is noticing the present moment.** His thought bubble reflects exactly where they are at that exact moment. He is taking in the sights, sounds, and beauty of the world around him. He is being mindful.

Give your child plenty of time to talk about and digest this idea. Feel free to fill in any details about the picture she may not have noticed.

GETTING STARTED

"Are You Mind Full or Mindful?" created by Henck van Bilsen, Cognitive Behavior Therapist and Clinical Psychologist at the Cognitive Behavior Therapy Partnership (CBT) in New Zealand

GETTING STARTED

MATERIALS NEEDED

Book
What Does It Mean to be Present? by Rana DiOrio

ACTIVITY 2: Read-Aloud: Introduce the Concept of Mindfulness

This book is my go-to book to introduce mindfulness to students. I suggest reading this as a part of the first lesson. It is written and illustrated in a way that encourages children to begin to embrace the idea that each moment is a gift. Living in the moment and being present for whatever happens is what mindfulness is all about.

MATERIALS NEEDED

- large clear jar
- glitter glue
- glitter shaker
- craft glue
- hot water

ACTIVITY 3: Clear Mind Jar

This activity is a great way for children to understand the meaning of having a full mind, like the boy in the picture from Activity One. It also represents how sitting quietly and paying attention to what is around or in front of us can help calm and refocus the mind and body.

To begin, squeeze one entire bottle of glitter glue into the jar (provided). Fill the jar with hot tap water. Stir the glue with a wire whisk or spoon or put the lid on tight and shake the jar until all the glitter glue dissolves. A bit of water may leak out of the top when you are shaking

GETTING STARTED

it, so you may want to have a towel at hand if this happens. Let the glitter in the jar settle before moving on to the next step.

Once the glitter has settled, ask your child if he remembers what the boy's mind was like in the picture. He may respond with something like, "He was thinking crazy thoughts" or he may refer to the emotions the child was experiencing: He was sad, excited, or worried. Talk a bit more about what a person's mind might become full of. A mind can be full of thoughts of anger, excitement, fear, worry, happiness or sadness, anything that takes our minds away from what is happening in the present moment.

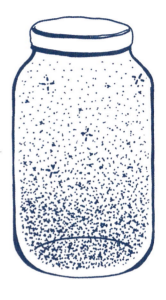

After you have this discussion with your child, show the jar and explain that the water in the jar represents our minds, and the glitter at the bottom of the jar represents our feelings and thoughts. Continue by explaining that when we wake up in the morning, before thoughts have had a chance to enter our minds, our mind is typically clear, like the water in the jar. As our day gets started and thoughts and emotions enter our minds, our minds begin to fill. Share an early morning thought of your own as you take the lid off of the jar and shake some glitter from the glitter shaker into the jar to represent that thought. Take turns listing thoughts that you or your child had that morning, and for each thought, shake some glitter into the jar. Some examples could be, "I wondered what I was going to have for breakfast," or "I was excited about my day," or maybe, "I wanted to stay in bed because I was tired and my bed was cozy."

GETTING STARTED

Clear Mind Jar (continued)

When you have listed several thoughts and put several shakes of glitter into the jar, put the lid back on and shake the jar vigorously. While shaking the jar, explain that these thoughts can distract us from noticing what is happening around us. Our thoughts, whether pleasurable or difficult, can also cloud our minds and make it hard to settle and concentrate. When we are angry or overly excited, our minds are extra "swirly," and it can be difficult to make good choices or respond to others in a respectful way. Before setting down the jar, tell your child that once you place the jar on the floor, both of you will sit quietly without saying anything. Place the jar down and focus your attention on the glitter (thoughts and emotions) in the jar. Explain that your job is to watch the glitter settle as you sit in peace.

Once the jar has settled, ask how your child feels at that moment. You may hear, "I feel calm," or "I feel sleepy." I once heard a child say he felt like he was in the middle of a beautiful snowstorm and it made him feel peaceful.

Once this activity is over, you can keep the jar and use it as a tool to calm and refocus when needed. If you have created a calm space within your home, this is a great addition to that space.

Notes: To prevent leaks, seal the lid. Remove the lid and dry the rim of the jar with a towel. Run a line of craft glue around the lid and replace the lid securely on the jar. The glue will help prevent water from leaking out when you shake the jar.

Clear Mind Jar Stories

A parent once came to me several days after her son took his jar home from a camp at the studio where I taught yoga. She told me that the day before, they had been anticipating the arrival of their cousins and the little boy was bouncing around the house in excitement. She told her son he needed to calm down, but didn't refer to the jar. She didn't even remember that he had it! But the boy remembered. He quickly ran to his bedroom, where his mother found him several minutes later, sitting on the floor watching the glitter settle. Not wishing to interrupt, she said nothing and went back downstairs. After several more minutes, her son returned, calm and centered.

Another wonderful experience involved a second-grade boy who had difficulty controlling his anger while at school. During one of his angry moments, I invited him into my office, and together we assembled his own clear mind jar. We talked about what the glitter represented and how the jar could help him when he was angry. He kept the jar with him and used it several times a day to calm himself and let go of his angry feelings.

GETTING STARTED

 Tuning In to Sound

MATERIALS NEEDED

- percussion chime

This activity can be done in a chair or in a seated position on the floor. Finding a comfortable position that can be held until the activity is over is important. If you are practicing in a chair, ask your child to sit "back to back, seat to seat" before beginning breathing exercises. This means sitting with her spine to the back of the chair and her seat comfortably on the seat of the chair. This will encourage good posture and will allow her lungs to expand fully. Slouching or leaning forward will constrict the lungs and impede airflow. If your child is on the floor and space permits, encourage her to sit or lie down in a comfortable position that will allow her to complete the exercise with minimal fidgeting. Remember, the goal is to focus on the breath rather than discomforts that might come from not practicing her best posture.

Take out the percussion chime from the kit and sound the chime so your child can hear how the sound resonates. Ask her to raise her hand when she can no longer hear the sound. Then sound the chime a second time as closure. Now ask her to close her eyes and repeat the same activity. Discuss how closing the eyes can make the sense of hearing more acute.

GETTING STARTED

Once your child has experienced the activity with eyes closed, sound the chime one last time. Instruct her to slowly open her eyes when she can no longer hear the sound. Ask your child how she feels at that moment. You will most likely hear the words "calm," "peaceful," "quiet," "sleepy," and maybe even "wonderful." Keep in mind that not every child will feel calm and peaceful right away. In fact, some children may say they felt nervous or anxious. If this occurs, explain that feeling nervous or anxious is perfectly natural. Reassure your child that it does take time to become comfortable with the part of mindfulness in which we turn our focus inward. However, the more she practices, the easier it should become.

If you have created a calm space within your home, the percussion chime is a great addition to that space.

GETTING STARTED

 ## Gratitude Chains

I do this as an introductory activity because once it's taught, children can add new links to their chain whenever they feel the urge and watch it grow with gratitude.

Use whatever type of paper you have. I like to use colored paper because it makes the chain more enjoyable to look at. White paper can also work well, if you are using colored markers or crayons. The strips can be taped or stapled together to make the chain.

When young children develop their gratitude chain, it's important to focus on the idea, not the execution. Correct spelling or perfect handwriting should not be the main focus. Your child may draw what he is grateful for if that is the stage of development he's in. It's important to keep in mind that the chains belong to your child and all that matters is that he himself understands them.

To begin the activity, talk about what being grateful means and share a few examples of what your child may be grateful for. Some ideas:

- the sound of the birds outside his bedroom window
- the warm sun on his skin.
- Mother Earth
- flowers

MATERIALS NEEDED

- colored strips of paper about 1-inch wide
- markers

GETTING STARTED

- the food in his belly
- the puddles on the street
- the blanket on his bed
- his family
- his pet
- the ability to run on the playground or in the yard
- his friends

This list of ideas typically creates conversation and presents an opportunity to point out the difference between wants and needs. Show your child the chain strips and explain that he can think of ideas to put on the chain.

Limit the number of strips to two or three per day and only one idea per strip. If they have the opportunity to fill out as many strips as they want, or write down many ideas at once, children tend to lose sight of the purpose of the activity. If coming up with ideas proves to be difficult, use a meal time to brainstorm ideas or use the time spent together in the car as a chance to look around at all the beauty that surrounds you. If the entire family wants to get involved, you can make one family chain and hang it in a common place in your home to remind everyone of the great things in their lives.

Now that you've completed the introductory activities, you're ready to move on. The remainder of the activities in this book are organized into six categories that address key elements in mindfulness practice. Feel free to choose activities that meet the needs — and moods — of your child from any of the following sections.

Breath Work: breath awareness, relaxation and breath control

 Using the Five Senses: self-awareness, exploration of surroundings, observation and making connections

 Gratitude: appreciation for others and the surrounding world, optimism, increased positivity, and finding the good in negative situations

 Kindness: greater respect for others, sense of belonging, improved self-esteem, and overall happiness as a result of doing kind deeds

 Empathy: altruism, expression, recognition of emotion, social awareness, and awareness of the conscience

 Togetherness: participation, sense of community, leadership, trust in others, friendship, problem-solving, communication, and teamwork

Mindful Breathing Activities

Breathing in, I calm my body.
Breathing out, I smile.
Dwelling in the present moment,
I know this is a wonderful moment.
– Thich Nhat Hanh

Breath work is a key component of mindfulness practice. We need to understand that our breath is a bridge between our mind and our body. We breathe all day, every day, usually without thinking about it. In mindful breathing, we take a moment to pay attention to our inhalations and exhalations. Mindful attention to the breath helps us learn to notice when thoughts and feelings arise, and thereby lessen the times our thoughts draw us into stories and mind-wandering. Concentrating on our breath brings us back to the present moment. The less we worry about what will happen, or ruminate about what has happened, the closer we move toward a healthy mind and a calm, grounded body.

A Few Tips Before Practicing Breathing Activities

These activities provide your child with the opportunity to become more aware of her body. Recognition of the breath can help her to self-regulate emotions and refocus. Practicing deep breathing brings a rush of oxygen to the cells, leaving those who practice with less anxiety and stress. It also helps to control anger, depression and frustration while leaving the body calm and energized.

Here are a few things to keep in mind before beginning breath work with your child:

- These breathing activities are best experienced with eyes closed. However, closing the eyes can be uncomfortable or frightening for some children, or for children who have undergone trauma. Encourage doing these activities with eyes closed, but allow your child the freedom to keep his eyes open, with the gaze soft and downward toward the tip of the nose or floor. You can explain this by instructing him to soften his face and his jaw. Once the face relaxes, the gaze soon follows. I like to tell children that a soft gaze feels the way it feels when you are sleepy, right before your eyes close.

- Unless otherwise noted, breathing activities are practiced by breathing in and out through the nose.

- If you plan to incorporate yoga poses into your breath work, the general rule is to breathe in (inhale) with rising, expanding motions and to breathe out (exhale) with lowering, contracting motions.

- You will notice that some activities ask your child to hold her breath for several counts. This is to practice breath control. The actual counts aren't as important as the practice of stopping the breath for a brief amount of time.

- Once taught, these activities can be used at any time of the day, in a group setting or alone. If you or your child feel the need to calm the mind and body, pick one and give it a try.

MINDFUL BREATHING

Breathing In, Breathing Out: 1

PURPOSE

calming

MATERIALS NEEDED

none needed

This easy activity takes just a minute and can be done in a comfortable seated position. It is great for the beginner and is a nice introduction to the practice of observing the breath and noticing thoughts that come and go. Also, it's a great activity for any of us when we need a break throughout our day.

Focusing on the breath without becoming distracted is an almost-impossible task. Our minds are constantly active, even when we sleep. It's natural to lose focus on the breath and think of other things. An important part of breath work is simply noticing any thoughts that come into our minds, acknowledging them, then letting them go and bringing the focus back to the breath.

You can keep this simple when explaining to your child. Before we practice for the first time, I tell children that we are only going to think about breathing in and breathing out. If they start to think of anything else, they can simply recognize that thought and right away try to go back to thinking about their breath.

MINDFUL BREATHING

If this seems difficult for your child, you could encourage the use of anchor words, which helps to regulate his breath. For example, on each inhalation, your child can say to himself silently, "I'm breathing in." As he exhales, "I'm breathing out." Try it together for one minute. At the end of this activity share your answers to the following questions:

- **How do you feel?**

- **Was this easy or hard to do?**

- **Were you able to stay focused on your breath or did you notice your mind wandering?**

- **If your mind wandered, were you able to bring your attention back to your breath?**

Body Scan

PURPOSE

body awareness

MATERIALS NEEDED

none

This activity can be done in a comfortable seated position, or lying down. Invite your child to start at the crown (top) of the head and think about how this part of their body feels. As she focuses on her crown, have her say the word "calm" in her mind after each exhalation. Guide her down her body by softly calling out the body parts at right. You could instruct her like this:

"Sit in a comfortable seated position and close your eyes or soften your gaze by relaxing your face and jaw. Think about the top of your head. As you let your breath go, or exhale, say the word "calm" in your mind as you relax the top of your head. Now move to your forehead, and as you exhale, say the word "calm" in your mind as you relax your forehead."

Work your way down through your child's cheeks, jaw, shoulders, upper arms, lower arms, fingers, belly, hips, upper legs, lower legs, toes and feet.

Very young children can eliminate the thinking of the word "calm." They can just think about the part of the body you are referring to as they exhale. If this is still too advanced, just invite your child to think about each body part without focusing on her breath.

MINDFUL BREATHING

Activity 3: Four-Corner Breath

PURPOSE

calming

MATERIALS NEEDED

none

To begin, show your child the square diagram on the opposite page and model the breathing described below while tracing the square with your finger. Once your child understands the idea, invite him to sit in a comfortable seated position. Guide him to close his eyes or soften his gaze and picture a square in his mind.

Have your child focus on one corner of his imaginary square and inhale as you count to four, moving his attention along his imaginary square to the next corner. Instruct him to hold his breath and keep his focus on the corner as you count to four again. As he exhales, he moves his focus to the next corner for a count of four. At that corner, he holds for a count of four. He inhales to the count of four as he travels to the next corner. Again, he holds his breath at the corner for four counts, and exhales as he travels to the final corner to complete the square.

Return to normal breathing after one or two rounds.

MINDFUL BREATHING

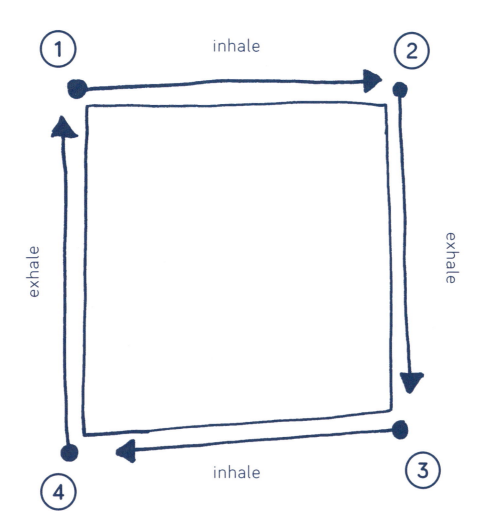

MINDFUL BREATHING

Activity 4: High Five

PURPOSE

calming

MATERIALS NEEDED

none

This can be done in a comfortable seated position, or lying down. If sitting, your child should place her hands in her lap. If lying down, she may rest her hands, palms down, on the belly or floor. Instruct your child to inhale while counting "one, two, three, four, five" in her mind, pause briefly, then exhale while counting to five. This is considered one round. Have her do this five times, keeping track of each round by pressing each finger of one hand into her lap, belly or floor.

When your child has gone through five rounds, she is done with the exercise. If she wants or needs more, she can use both hands to count ten rounds.

MINDFUL BREATHING

Activity 5: Filling the Balloon

This can be done sitting or standing. Your child begins by taking little "sips" of air to slowly fill his belly, imagining he is blowing up a balloon as his belly expands. He should continue to take sips until the "balloon" is full and he can no longer take in any more air. Then, he can exhale as he bends over, letting all the air in his belly escape forcefully — as though the balloon has been released and has flown from his hands.

PURPOSE

This exercise is both energizing and calming and makes a nice transition between exercise and becoming settled.

MATERIALS NEEDED

none

MINDFUL BREATHING

ACTIVITY 6: What Type Are You?

PURPOSE

body awareness/centering

MATERIALS NEEDED

none

We all breathe differently. Some breathe more from the chest and some breathe more from the belly. The difference is determined by the movement of the diaphragm. The diaphragm's purpose is to draw air into the lungs by increasing the capacity of the thoracic cavity. The "chest breath" occurs when, on inhalation, the diaphragm lifts the lower end of the rib cage and sternum. The "belly breath" occurs when, on inhalation, the diaphragm presses down into the abdominal cavity, which allows for the belly to expand. Both types of breathing can happen in isolation or they can happen simultaneously. Belly breathing, or deep breathing, can trigger the body's natural relaxation response and can help alleviate stress and anxiety, among other things. This is a nice activity to build your child's awareness of her body and help her understand what type of breather she is.

I suggest doing this in a comfortable seated position. Ask your child to place one hand on her belly and the other hand on her chest. Invite her to close her eyes if she wishes, and focus on her breath for one minute. Encourage her to take notice of where she feels expansion or

MINDFUL BREATHING

growth as she inhales. Does she feel the movement more in the chest or belly? As she exhales, which area compresses or shrinks?

Option: This exercise can also be done lying down. If you do the exercise both sitting and lying down, ask your child whether she noticed a difference in the way she breathed in each position.

Activity 7: Belly Breathing: Sitting

This version of belly breathing is best done in a comfortable seated position. Your child should rest his hands on his belly. With eyes closed, he breathes in and expands the belly to its fullest, then exhales, while eliminating all the air, shrinking the belly back to its normal size. I like to tell young children to imagine filling a big beach ball as they breathe in, then imagine letting the air out of the ball as they breathe out. Repeat several times.

PURPOSE

body awareness/centering

MATERIALS NEEDED

none

MINDFUL BREATHING

Activity 8: Heart Breath

PURPOSE

heart-warming

MATERIALS NEEDED

none

This is a great exercise to do with your child during the gratitude or kindness lessons. This is best done in a comfortable seated position. Have your child place her hands on her heart or make a heart sign with her hands. Then have her imagine she's drawing her breath in through the front of the heart as she inhales and releases it out the back as she exhales. You can encourage her to send kind thoughts to others while doing this. For example, you could say, "As you breathe in, send kind thoughts to yourself. As you breathe out, send kind thoughts to your brother, sister, friend, etc."

MINDFUL BREATHING

Activity 9: Buzzing Like a Bee

Encourage your child to sit in a comfortable seated position either in a chair or on the floor. This activity requires him to constrict the back of his throat to create a low buzzing sound, which may be difficult to understand. Before beginning this activity, practice by asking your child to lift the back of his tongue to the back of his throat while he exhales to make the low buzzing sound.

Have your child cover his eyes with his fingers and close his ears with his thumbs. Then, keeping his lips closed and teeth slightly apart, ask him to inhale deeply to the count of four while closing off his throat just slightly so he can hear his breath. Have him exhale slowly through the mouth to the count of four while making a low buzzing sound like a bee. Repeat three times.

PURPOSE

self-awareness

MATERIALS NEEDED

none

MINDFUL BREATHING

PURPOSE

self-awareness

MATERIALS NEEDED

none

 Robot Hands

Ask your child to extend her arms in front of her at shoulder level, with palms facing toward each other. Have her breathe in deeply through her nose for a count of four as she slowly moves her arms out to either side. Then, instruct her to exhale fully through her mouth for a count of four as she brings her hands together in front again. Challenge her to see how close she can bring her palms together without touching. Repeat three times.

PURPOSE

calming/refocusing

MATERIALS NEEDED

- Hoberman Sphere

 Breathing In, Breathing Out: 2

I prefer to do this activity while seated, but it can also be done in a standing position. Ask your child to place his hands on his belly. Then slowly expand the Hoberman sphere, instructing him to inhale at the same rate, finishing the in-breath when the sphere is fully open. As you contract the sphere slowly, have him exhale, finishing the out-breath when the sphere is fully contracted. Repeat as needed.

Options: After your child inhales fully, have him hold his breath for three counts. Then tell him to release his breath slowly as you contract the sphere. Repeat. If you have created a calm space within your home, the Hoberman sphere is a great addition to that space.

MINDFUL BREATHING

ACTIVITY 12: Calming Breath

This can be done seated or standing. If using bubbles, be sure to take this activity outdoors. Ask your child to take a slow, deep breath, then hold the breath for three counts. Release the breath by blowing the pinwheel or bubble wand. Repeat three times.

Option: Invite your child to repeat this activity using exhalations of different intensities. What does she notice when she exhales forcefully? Are there more or fewer bubbles? Does the pinwheel move faster or slower? What type of exhalations give them the most control over the bubbles or pinwheels?

PURPOSE

calming

MATERIALS NEEDED

- pinwheels or bubbles

MINDFUL BREATHING

Activity 13: Noticing What You Notice

PURPOSE

calming/
self-regulation

MATERIALS NEEDED

- feathers

This is a breath-control activity that can be done either seated or standing. The purpose of experiencing breath control is not simply to control the breath, but to notice its effects. Tuning into our breathing can induce relaxation of our mind and body.

Have your child hold the feather in one hand in front of her. Guide her to inhale deeply, then blow along one side of the feather for a count of three, starting at the base and stopping when she reaches the tip of the feather. Ask if she could control her breath so she was at the top of the feather when you reached the count of three. Repeat, instructing her this time to blow down along the other side of the feather as you count to three. Again, check in on how she did. Try this several more times to see if practice has made her better able to control her breath.

MINDFUL BREATHING

Activity 14: Belly Breathing: Lying Down

Let your child pick a favorite stuffed animal to use for this activity. Have him lie on his back and place his stuffed animal on his belly. Tell him he's going to take his animal on a ride on the ocean waves and that his breath is going to create the waves. As he inhales and expands his belly to its fullest, the animal rises on a "wave" of breath. As he exhales, the belly softens as the wave passes. Repeat as needed.

PURPOSE

body awareness/calming

MATERIALS NEEDED

- small stuffed animal

MINDFUL BREATHING

Activity 15: Praticing Breath Control

This works well at a table or on the floor. Give your child a straw and a pom-pom. Have him touch one end of the straw to the pom-pom. Ask him to exhale fully through his nose. On his next inhalation, have him breathe deeply through the straw and try to lift the pom-pom off the table or floor using the suction created by his breath. Once he has mastered this, challenge him to try holding the pom-pom to the straw with his breath for a count of three before exhaling and letting it drop.

Options: You can add a count or two to the inhalation on each repetition. To avoid dizziness, don't exceed a count of six. Or challenge your child to match the inhalation with the exhalation. For example, if inhaling for a count of three, guide him through a three-count exhalation.

PURPOSE

energizing

MATERIALS NEEDED

- straws
- pom-poms

Affirmations

An affirmation is a positive statement of encouragement that is said to oneself. Introducing your child to the power of affirmations can help develop self-acceptance, self-worth and confidence. The older we get, the harder it becomes to take ownership of our good traits because we aren't used to complimenting ourselves and vocalizing our greatness. Affirmations are best done out loud, or even in front of a mirror. If your child is not ready to vocalize affirmations, they can be practiced during quiet sitting by saying them softly or by thinking them. There is no right or wrong way to practice. A child may start with saying an affirmation several times and then work up to a longer stretch. Research supports the power of positive affirmations. When practiced regularly and with good intent, affirmations strengthen neural connections in the brain. I have listed a few affirmations that are good starting points, but feel free to make up your own!

- I am wonderful.
- I like myself the way I am.
- I am beautiful inside and out.
- I am loved and I love others.
- I try my hardest.
- I am a good friend.
- I am grateful and compassionate.
- I choose to be happy.
- I don't know it yet, so I'll keep trying.
- I am respectful and kind.

Mudras for Children

Children love mudras! Mudras are a symbols made with the hands that tune us into the subtle energies of the body. Our fingertips have many nerve endings and pressing them together to form a symbol or shape can be very calming, healing or even energizing. Mudras can be used for self-regulation and body awareness and are typically done in a seated position. Once you have introduced your child to the breathing activities in this book, you can introduce a mudra to use if she is ready to move on to quiet sitting. These are three of my favorite mudras to use when working with children.

1. Grounding mudra
Good to do with excited and energized children to help calm and find peace. This mudra is also known as the Gyan Mudra, which means wisdom and knowledge. Keep the arms straight and the back of the hands resting on the knees, Touch the index finger and thumb together to make a circle. The remaining three fingers fall naturally open.

2. Mudra to encourage a growth mindset and confidence

Do this with your child when he feels frustrated or you sense a lack of self-confidence. This is also a great mudra to do with children with ADD/ADHD.

Loosely interlock the fingers of both hands together and turn your hands so one thumb is facing up and the other down. Hands rest in the lap. Your child can repeat "I can do it" or "I got this" silently while sitting in this pose. This mudra is named for Ganesha, who is the Hindu god considered to be the remover of obstacles in that faith.

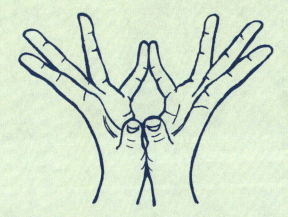

3. Mudra for kindness

The hand gesture that means loving kindness is called the Padma Mudra. It's also known as the lotus. This provides an opening to release and accept kindness. It also helps calm and ground.

Press the base of the hands and the tips of the pinky fingers and thumbs together. Let the index, middle and ring finger float outwards to represent the lotus petals. Imagine light or kind thoughts coming out of the center of the flower.

Exploring the Five Senses

I go to nature to be soothed and healed, and to have my senses put in order.
– JOHN BURROUGHS

It's delightful to watch as a young baby uses its senses to learn about itself and the world. He slowly and mindfully brings his fingers into view to make sense out of those strange objects floating in front of him. Her lips pucker

when she's introduced to a sour food. What happens when she hears the sound of her mother's voice or a car abruptly honking its horn? Babies and young children have a beginner's mind: a mind that is fresh and new. A beginner's mind does not have preconceived ideas about anything. It experiences everything as if for the first time.

Babies learn about, explore and make sense of the world around them by using their ears, eyes, nose, mouth and skin. Many young children are exposed to sensory play in their early years of development to strengthen the neural pathways. This group of activities — exploring sight, sound, smell, taste, and touch — will encourage children to learn about, appreciate and connect to their world.

Smell

If only there could be an invention that bottled up a memory, like scent. And it never faded, and it never got stale. And then, when one wanted it, the bottle could be uncorked, and it would be like living the moment all over again.
—Daphne du Maurier

When scent enters our nostrils, it passes by special receptors that have the ability to differentiate between thousands of smells. Once identified, a smell can provide a great deal of information about the environment. Because our brains can associate certain smells with particular people or places, scents can often trigger powerful memories. Ask your child if they know of smells that trigger positive or negative memories. Someone may say they love the smell of coffee because it reminds them of a significant adult, or that they love the smell of rain because it reminds them of summertime. A child once told me he hated the smell of wet plastic because it reminded him of the time he camped for a weekend in the rain. Explore some of the following experiences and the power of smell.

THE FIVE SENSES: SMELL

Mindful Walk

MATERIALS NEEDED

- a beautiful place to walk

Take your child outdoors on a walk in a quiet space. Parks or nature trails make great places for a mindful walk. Encourage your child to be quiet as she walks, and to use her sense of smell to take in all the scents that surround her. Invite her to smell the flowers and plants she passes; even the leaves and bark of trees have a smell. Pick up a handful of dirt and smell its earthiness.

Take a moment at the end of the walk to sit quietly together and talk about how it felt to focus on the scents surrounding her. What did she notice that she might not have noticed before?

Option: Bring along paper and a writing utensil so your child can write or draw what she smells. Recording her items on a piece of paper can aid in recalling her experience when you reflect.

THE FIVE SENSES: SMELL

ACTIVITY 2

No-Sew Eye Pillows With or Without Essential Oils

These easy-to-make eye pillows are great to use in your calm space or as an aid when going to sleep. These can also be used during any of the lying-down breathing activities. To make it a scent sensory activity and aid in the relaxation of the eyes, body and mind, add a drop or two of essential oil. You can purchase all-natural essential oils online or at your local health food store.

To make the eye pillows, find a long sock that your child may already have in his drawer — or pick out a pair of colorful, fun socks at the store and make two! Have your child hold the opening of the sock open as you pour one to two cups of rice into the sock. If you are using essential oils, add a drop or two to the rice at this point. Tie a knot near the opening of the sock, leaving about two inches of the top exposed. Younger children will need help from an adult to tie the sock.

MATERIALS NEEDED

- large tube sock
- rice
- essential oils (optional)
- measuring cup

THE FIVE SENSES: SMELL

No-Sew Eye Pillows With or Without Essential Oils (continued)

If you chose to use oils, shake the sock to disperse the oils. Then shift all the rice to the tied end of the sock and tie a second knot on the toe end so the knot rests near the heel of the sock, disguising the heel. This will leave about two inches exposed on the other end so the ends match and the pillow will rest evenly on the eyes. If using oils, you may find the smell is too strong at first. If this is the case, let the finished eye pillows sit for a few hours or overnight before placing on the eyes.

THE FIVE SENSES: SMELL

Activity 3: What's That Smell?

Blindfold your child and let him smell the fragrant items you have collected. Don't let him touch the items, as touching them may give away the identity of the fragrance.

Afterward, take a moment to talk about how it felt to use only the sense of smell. Was it difficult or easy to identify the scent while blindfolded?

MATERIALS NEEDED

- fragrant items that your child is familiar with, such as pine needles, mint, cinnamon, vanilla, or lemon
- containers to hold the items
- blindfold

Touch

*Touch comes before sight, before speech. It is the
first language and the last, and it always tells the truth.*
— Margaret Atwood

We thrive on our sense of touch: the warm feel of a hand as it slips into yours, the burn on the soles of the feet as they connect with the hot sand on a beach, the sharp bite of the wind shifting just before a storm. We learn so much about ourselves and the world around us through our sense of touch. Touch is one of the easiest senses to experience mindfully. Use the following activities to help develop your child's sense of touch and aid in enhancing his body- and self-awareness.

THE FIVE SENSES: TOUCH

Activity 1: Partner Drawing

MATERIALS NEEDED

none

This is a simple and quiet game that a child of any age can enjoy. Since this is a partner activity, do this with your child or add in a sibling or friend. Sit so one person is facing the other's back. The first person will draw shapes, letters, or full words (depending on the age of the players) on the other's back. The second person must guess what the other person is drawing or writing. Ask your child to try closing her eyes as she guesses. Does that help? Switch partners.

THE FIVE SENSES: TOUCH

 Texture Rubbings

To do this activity, you will need access to textured surfaces, such as tiles, carpeting, braille signs, wood, baskets, tree bark, leaves, playground equipment, or rocks.

Texture is all around us. A beautiful way to experience the various textures of the world around us is through texture rubbings. Look around with your child to find textured objects indoors or out. Children may see many different types of textures that adults may miss.

Place a piece of paper over the textured surface and rub the paper lightly with the side of a crayon until the texture appears on the paper. This is fun to do outside during all the seasons of the year since so much of nature changes from season to season.

MATERIALS NEEDED

- crayons
- paper
- a variety of textured surfaces

THE FIVE SENSES: TOUCH

The Beauty of the Heartbeat

MATERIALS NEEDED

none

This is a quick and peaceful activity that can help calm down an anxious or excited child. It also helps your child become aware of how his body is working and reacting to the world around him.

Begin in a comfortable seated position with eyes closed or partially closed. If you are able, dim the lights in the room. Ask your child to place his right hand on his heart while inhaling and exhaling through his nose. As he sits quietly, have him tune into the beating of his heart. How does it feel? Can he feel the rate slowing the longer he sits?

Now, guide your child toward being aware of his clothes on his body. Can he feel the fabric touching his skin? Can he feel the chair or the floor beneath him? Are there areas of his body that feel uncomfortable at that moment? What area feels "just right," or comfortable? Ask him to share how this activity made him feel.

THE FIVE SENSES: TOUCH

ACTIVITY 4: Mystery Boxes

Before doing this activity, prepare the boxes by cutting a hole in each one big enough for a hand, but small enough so your child cannot easily see into the box. Place one object in each box. The goal is to have your child figure out what the object is using only his sense of touch. Hand your child the first box and let him spend a moment feeling the object. He may share many guesses about what it could be. Talk through this with him. Ask: is it hard or soft? Does it feel heavy? As he works through the boxes, have him close his eyes and ask if closing off his sense of sight makes his sense of touch more acute. After your child has had a chance to figure out all the boxes, have him hide items in the boxes for *you* to figure out!

MATERIALS NEEDED

- three to four shoe boxes with lids
- random items of different textures and sizes

Hearing

The quieter you become, the more you can hear.
– Author unknown

Listening mindfully to sounds is a powerful way to notice what is happening in the present moment. Once your child is introduced to this practice, it can be performed at any time of the day to help center and calm the body. Practicing mindful listening activities can help clear the mind of clutter and can help promote inner stillness.

THE FIVE SENSES: HEARING

Tuning In to What's Around Us: Indoors

MATERIALS NEEDED

- percussion chime

Find a comfortable seated position either in a chair or on the floor. Begin the activity by mentioning that sounds are always all around us, and that most of the time we are too busy to notice them. Tell your child that she will be sitting mindfully for about a minute and her job is to listen to the sounds around her. Invite her to close her eyes if she wishes, then sound the chime. After about a minute has passed, sound the chime again as the cue to open her eyes.

Talk about what your child heard. Point out all the sounds she most likely hadn't noticed before. Perhaps she heard the dishwasher running, or cars passing outside. Maybe she heard a TV from another room, or the wind blowing against the house.

Hint: As with any timed activity, use your judgment to decide how long your child will sit. A younger child may have difficulty sitting for a minute, while someone older may want more time.

THE FIVE SENSES: HEARING

Activity 2: Tuning In to What's Around Us: Outdoors

I like to repeat this activity during different seasons of the year because each season brings many different sounds. Take your child outside and find a quiet place to sit. Encourage him to sit in a comfortable seated position wherever he is and to close his eyes and listen for a time you feel is reasonable. You can bring the percussion chime with you if you wish to use it to cue the beginning and ending of the time you spend listening.

Discuss what you heard. Ask your child to identify sounds he may not have noticed if he hadn't been sitting mindfully with his eyes closed. Sounds he may mention: the wind blowing past his ears, a car honking or driving by, birds chirping, leaves swirling.

MATERIALS NEEDED

- percussion chime (optional)

THE FIVE SENSES: HEARING

Activity 3: Musical Mandalas

MATERIALS NEEDED

- music of choice
- mandala coloring book
- colored pencils or markers
- pencil
- ruler

Mandalas are circular, detailed drawings that represent cultures from all over the world. Mandala designs are used as a form of visual meditation to allow for self-discovery, relaxation and healing. When coloring mandalas, I find it most effective to find a quiet space with few distractions. Practicing a calm breathing activity together before you begin can also be helpful in turning off the ever-chattering mind, and gives time for the mind and body to settle. Pick out music to match the mood of the moment and invite your child listen to the tone, melody and tempo of the music.

The mandalas provided in the kit are suitable for all ages. But if your child is feeling more creative, he may prefer to draw his own to color.

Some helpful tips when drawing mandalas:

- Since mandalas are circular in shape, have your child start by drawing a large circle on the paper as the outline.

- Using the ruler, lightly draw a line to divide the circle in half one way then draw a second line to divide it in half the other way. This will make four quadrants so the designs can be added symmetrically.

- Starting in the middle, add a small circle where the two lines intersect. Moving outward from this circle, add lines, swirls, and

THE FIVE SENSES: HEARING

shapes in each quadrant. Mandalas are typically symmetrical, but since this is your child's work, let him explore and create a mandala that is uniquely his.

Musical Drawing

Find a quiet space in your home and offer your child some paper and writing utensils of her choice. Let her know she will spend the next few minutes drawing to music. Tell her she doesn't have to draw a masterpiece, she just needs to feel the music and to go where the music takes her.

Emphasize that this is not a coloring or drawing activity, but a listening activity. Your child doesn't have to be a great artist. The purpose is to calm the mind by focusing on the music while she draws.

Start the music and invite your child to draw with the rhythm and tempo of the music. You can decide how long to let the music play. After you stop the music, take a moment to ask how your child feels. Hang your child's artwork in your calm space or somewhere else in the home as a reminder of the peace she felt doing this activity.

MATERIALS NEEDED

- calm music
- paper
- writing utensils

Sight

Above all, watch with glittering eyes the whole world around you because the greatest secrets are always hidden in the most unlikely places.

– Roald Dahl, from Charlie and the Chocolate Factory

Sight is probably the sense we take most for granted. We use our sight to navigate through our lives and rarely take the time to slow down and notice the little things happening around us each day: birds flying overhead, the colors of the sunrise, or the deep brown color of the eyes of a friend. These activities will help your child focus on the present by slowing down and appreciating the visual details around her. Teaching our children to be grateful for the earth's beauty is rewarding since many children are still looking through child eyes and are more able than adults to notice the little things.

THE FIVE SENSES: SIGHT

 ## What Do You Remember?

MATERIALS NEEDED

- random items from your home

Before beginning this activity, gather random objects from around your home and arrange the items on a table or other place where you can cover them.

The purpose of this activity is to see how much we remember when we really focus on what we see. Begin by explaining that you have set out a number of objects and that you will give your child about 30 seconds to study them. Once the time is up, you will cover the items.

Your child will then try to remember as many objects as he can. He can do this verbally or he can write or draw his answers. Afterwards, switch roles and try guessing what your child has hidden under the cover.

Hint: For younger children, put out fewer objects and let them study the objects for a longer period of time. For older children, add objects to increase the challenge.

THE FIVE SENSES: SIGHT

Mindful Walk

Take your child outdoors on a walk to a quiet space, such as a park or nature trail or even your school playground. Encourage her to remain quiet as you walk and to use her sense of sight to take in all the beauty that surrounds her. Give examples of little things she could miss if she were not taking the time to slow down: the clouds in the sky, a leaf dangling from a tree, a pebble lying on the ground, the brown grass at the edge of the sidewalk.

Take a moment at the end of the walk to sit quietly with your child and talk about what it felt like to focus on the beauty surrounding her. What did she notice that perhaps she wouldn't have noticed before?

MATERIALS NEEDED

- a beautiful place to walk

THE FIVE SENSES: SIGHT

Rainbow Walk

MATERIALS NEEDED

- a beautiful place to walk

This is another version of the mindful walk. The only difference is that during this walk, you will identify all of the colors of the rainbow in order. For example, first you will need to find something red. After you find something red, then you can find something orange. Then find the rest of the colors of the rainbow in order (yellow, green, blue, purple). The fun part of this walk is that you can't move on to the next color until you have found the previous one. This can allow for a nice long walk with your child.

Option: Bring your camera along to take pictures of the colors you find.

THE FIVE SENSES: SIGHT

ACTIVITY 4: Cloud Watch

MATERIALS NEEDED

- a sunny day with fluffy clouds and a place to watch them pass by

Take your child outside on a sunny day to watch the clouds. Depending on the location, you can lie in the grass or sit. Encourage your child to focus on one cloud and watch it over a period of time as it slowly changes shape. Do the clouds take any familiar shapes? Watch along with your child and point out a cloud you notice taking shape. Can each of you see what the other sees?

Taste

Mindful eating is very pleasant. We sit beautifully. We are aware of the people surrounding us. We are aware of the food on our plates. This is a deep practice.
– Thich Nhat Hanh

Exploring the sense of taste can help us identify and make observations about the world around us. Our taste buds allow us to tell the difference between sweet, salty, sour, and bitter foods. The olfactory receptors in the nose work together with the taste buds to make it possible to experience the flavors of your favorite foods. In our crazy lives, it's easy to eat without thinking about what we are consuming, or why. These mindful eating activities can help your child slow down and experience the textures and flavors of food as well as notice the beauty of what is happening around him during meals.

THE FIVE SENSES: TASTE

Activity 1: Timed Meal

MATERIALS NEEDED

- food available at meal or snacktime

Do this activity when you have plenty of time to share a meal together with few distractions.

Time the meal for 20 to 30 minutes. Tell your child that you want her to try to try make her food last the entire time by eating mindfully. As she eats, encourage her to taste and describe the foods she's eating. Talk about this experience as you are doing it. Look around at your surroundings.

Is it warm and comforting? Quiet or loud? Do the surroundings affect your child's experience of the food?

Option: This can also be made into a more festive experience where your child helps to prepare the menu and environment. You may also try this both ways. Is the experience of mindful eating different during a regular meal than during a planned party meal? What are some differences?

THE FIVE SENSES: TASTE

ACTIVITY 2: Blindfolded Taste Test

DIRECTIONS

This is a fun way to experience mindful eating. Explain that your child will be tasting several foods while blindfolded and that you aren't going to tell him what the food is. He will have to guess. Have him taste a variety of foods that have different taste characteristics: sweet, salty, sour, spicy and bitter. After each food is given, discuss. What does your child think it was? Did it taste different while blindfolded?

MATERIALS NEEDED

- various types of food
- blindfolds

ACTIVITY 3: Mindful Tasting Using the Other Senses

Gather a few of the foods mentioned in the column to the right and place them in front of your child one at a time. Tell her she can't eat it until you say so.

Invite her to look at the food carefully, noticing its color, texture, and size. Talk about what she sees.

MATERIALS NEEDED

- apple or peach slices, cranberries, raw vegetables, cubes of cheese, chocolate square or chips

THE FIVE SENSES: TASTE

Mindful Tasting Using the Other Senses (continued)

Next, have her smell the food, with eyes open and again with them closed. Can she describe the smell? Is it different or the same with eyes closed? How is her body reacting to the possibility of tasting it? Is her mouth watering? Is she excited because it's an appealing food? Or is she disappointed because it is not a favorite?

Now invite her to taste the food. Encourage her to chew slowly, taking notice of the temperature and texture of the food as well as its flavor. Did the texture change as she chewed it? Is the food sour, salty, or spicy? Encourage her to chew until the food becomes liquid in her mouths before swallowing.

As your child swallows, invite her to notice how the food feels as it slides down the throat. Can she feel it? Can she feel the food in her stomach? Repeat with the other foods you gathered.

Activity 4: Exploring All Five Senses

MATERIALS NEEDED
- marshmallows or gummy worms

Before beginning, explain to your child that he will be using all five senses for this activity. Hand him a marshmallow or gummy worm to explore. Talk through each sense as he experiences it. If he rushes through the activity on his own, the activity will lose its purpose.

80

THE FIVE SENSES: TASTE

Explore the food in the following order:

Sight: What does he see as he looks at the candy? Have him describe its color, shape, and size.

Touch: What does the candy feel like? Is it soft, gritty, lumpy? Ask your child to tear the candy in half and feel the inside. Is it the same? Different?

Smell: What does the candy smell like? Does the smell create any connections or provoke memories? Do the insides and outsides smell different?

Hearing: Does the candy make a sound when held still? Does it make a sound if moved around?

Taste: Finally! What does the candy taste like? Have your child taste with the tip of the tongue first. Then have him break a small amount off and place it in his mouth. Encourage him to roll the piece around on his tongue and to be mindful of the flavors. Before swallowing, have your child pinch his nostrils closed while the food is in his mouth. Does that change the taste?

Gratitude

Be thankful for what you have. Your life, no matter how bad you think it is, is someone else's fairytale.
— Wale Ayeni

When we feel gratitude we feel appreciation for what we have and possess the ability to look beyond what we want. Studies have shown that when gratitude is taught and incorporated into our lives, our level of well-being and happiness can increase. We live in a time where many have the mindset that "more" is better. Teaching gratitude as a life skill, or habit of mind, to children will allow them to notice and appreciate the simple pleasures in life.

If you are already doing the Gratitude Chains, use your judgment to decide if you want to add any of the following gratitude activities. I suggest introducing the Gratitude Journals (Activity Two) because these can be used privately and children can continue to journal their thoughts of gratitude on their own.

GRATITUDE

Activity 1: Pass the Gratitude

MATERIALS NEEDED

- Use an object that would be fun for children to pass. Perhaps a ball or a stuffed animal.

This is another activity that is done with a larger group of children or family members. Here, everyone sits a circle and passes the object from person to person. Whoever has the object says something he or she is grateful for.

Options: Play music while the object is passed around. Have someone in charge of starting and stopping the music. When the music stops, the person with the object says something they are grateful for. If outdoors, have those playing toss the object to each other. The game can also be played without an object; participants can share what they are grateful for simply by taking turns in the circle.

Activity 2: Gratitude Journals

MATERIALS NEEDED

- journal or notebook

Take a special shopping trip with your child to pick out a journal, or have him design one of his own by stapling paper together and decorating a cover however he chooses. This journal is for your child to write or draw what they are grateful for. It also can be used to record

GRATITUDE

thoughts, fears, dreams, etc. Since journals are typically personal, I suggest using these during a quiet time or at the end of the day to allow for peaceful reflection. If done with honesty and thought, journaling can be a beneficial habit for self-reflection and stress relief. You may soon notice your child journaling on her own without direction. You may also choose to experience these benefits, and model the importance of journaling by keeping your own journal.

ACTIVITY 3 Gratitude Jar

Each day, have your child write something he's grateful for on a slip of paper and place it in the jar. Invite all family members to do the same. Find a time that works for your family to share what's in the jar. Meals or before bed are great times to reflect on things you are all grateful for.

MATERIALS NEEDED

- large jar or container of your choice
- slips of paper
- pencils or markers

Kindness

People will forget what you said. People will forget what you did. But people will never forget how you made them feel.
– Maya Angelou

No one ever suffers from being kind to someone else. Spending a moment doing an act of kindness for someone else can change the path of both people's day. Children are born being kind. As they grow, they learn from others around them how to act and behave.

KINDNESS

 Activity 1: Kindness Hearts

MATERIALS NEEDED

- paper for making hearts
- scissors
- markers or crayons

This activity is a beautiful way to spread kindness to others. What I love about this one is that once you show your child how to do it, he can do it on his own when he recognizes the need to be kind to others.

Ask your child to think of several people for whom he would like to make a heart and to think of a phrase or word to put on the heart for each person. I like to brainstorm a list of kind words or short phrases such as: "I love you," "Peace," "Breathe," "Be happy," "Smile," "Thanks," "You are wonderful," "You are awesome." If writing is difficult, a kind picture works just fine. Drawings could include a flower, a smiley face, or any other cheerful image.

Next, show your child how to make and cut out paper hearts from paper you have. Making two or three is a good start. Once his hearts are cut out he can then write or draw his message on the heart. Encourage him to place the heart in an area where it will be found when your child isn't there. For example, he could place a heart that says, "I love you" on his mother's pillow, or a heart that says, "Smile" on the seat of his father's car so he sees it on his way to work. He could put a heart that says, "You are wonderful" in the mailbox of an elderly neighbor. The possibilities are endless. Remind your child to keep the hearts a secret so they are a surprise when found.

KINDNESS

Talk with your child about how he thinks his special people will respond when they find their hearts. Watch his joy when that special person responds in a loving and grateful way.

ACTIVITY 2: Thinking Kind Acts

This is a breathing activity. Encourage a comfortable seated position before beginning. Ask your child to breathe in deeply through the nose as you count to four. As he breathes, he should imagine doing a kind act for someone, and try to picture that thought as a cloud bubble above his own head. He will then let the cloud drift away as he breathes out fully through the mouth for a count of four. Repeat three times, inviting him to imagine a different kind act each time.

Option: Sending Kind Wishes

If the Thinking Kind Acts activity is too difficult for your child, or if you want another variation, try this. Sending Kind Wishes is a quiet, personal activity that helps calm the mind and body. Ask your child to come to a comfortable seated position on the floor or a chair and close his eyes, if he chooses. Invite your child to think kind thoughts and use his imagination to send the thoughts to people or animals he loves or cares about.

MATERIALS NEEDED

none

KINDNESS

Thinking Kind Acts (continued)

Some examples to get your child started:

• Send a kind thought to your teacher and tell him you can't wait to see him the next day.

• Send a kind thought to a brother or sister and wish them luck on an upcoming event.

• Send a kind thought to grandparents and let them know that you love them and are thinking of them.

Of course, the recipients of these kind thoughts don't know that they are getting them. The purpose of this activity is to generate peace and kindness within your child, which in turn, encourages him to spread kindness and compassion to others. Expect to feel a beautiful calmness radiate from your child after this activity.

KINDNESS

Activity 3: Peace Flags

Peace flags can serve as gentle reminders that we all need to work together to bring peace to the world. This is an activity to do with more than one child, so invite a few friends over. Each will receive a section of the flag to decorate, but in the end, the pieces will be strung together to represent spreading peace as a community.

Begin this activity by asking the kids to brainstorm a list of things or symbols that make them feel at peace. Ideas could include rivers or streams, peace symbols, clouds, birds, rain, fireplaces, or a hug from someone special. If you have paper, you may want to let children sketch their ideas before drawing on the cardboard.

Once each child has completed their section, create a group peace flag by stringing the twine through the holes at the top of each piece of cardboard. Children may want to take turns displaying the flag at their houses so all their families can appreciate it.

MATERIALS NEEDED

- tag board or cardboard pieces with holes punched through the top (see picture)
- twine or string

KINDNESS

Kindness Bingo

Use the bingo board on the next page as is, or make copies for your child to share with friends or take along on a trip. Start by challenging your child to complete a row or column. You can also have her work towards a blackout, where the entire board is complete.

MATERIALS NEEDED

- bingo game board
- markers

KINDNESS

KINDNESS

B	I	N	G	O
Say hello to someone new to you.	Pick up garbage you see on the ground or floor.	Hold a door open for someone.	Walk with someone you usually don't walk with.	Give someone a hug.
Help someone carry something heavy.	Let someone go ahead of you in line.	Tell someone they are special.	Do something nice for yourself.	Play with someone new outside or on the playground.
Thank an adult for being there for you.	Share a treat with someone.	FREE	Smile at 6 new people today.	High-five a friend for no reason.
Give someone a compliment.	Really listen to what someone is saying to you.	Read a story to someone.	Apologize for something you did even if it was an accident.	Say thank you to a teacher or other adult.
Help prepare a snack or meal.	Help a friend with homework or a chore.	Play a game with someone.	Do something kind for the earth.	Notice a pet or other animal and give it some love.

KINDNESS

Acts of Kindness

MATERIALS NEEDED

- various materials depending on chosen activity

Share some of these ideas with your child or brainstorm a list of your own to demonstrate ways to show kindness.

1. Say "hello" to everyone you see today.

2. Donate books you no longer use to those in need.

3. Cut a snowflake from paper and give it to a special friend.

4. Hand write a letter and mail it to someone special.

5. Make a thank-you card for your mail carrier or bus driver.

6. Hold a door for someone even if you have to wait for them to catch up.

7. Ask someone how they are doing today and really listen to their response.

8. Smile at every single person you see for the entire day. You will probably get rewarded with smiles in return.

9. Let someone go ahead of you in line.

10. Help a neighbor or classmate out with a job.

KINDNESS

11. Bake a treat for someone and share it with them.

12. Help a teacher or parent do something you take for granted (wipe the tables, pick up the floor, make a snack).

13. Pick up trash you see on the ground. (Be sure to wash your hands afterwards.)

14. Sit with someone at school during lunch who looks lonely.

15. Give at least five compliments to others today.

16. Ask someone, "What can I do to help you today?"

17. Really listen to someone when they are talking to you. Be in the present and don't let your mind wander.

18. Offer to carry someone's backpack or other item they may be carrying.

19. Make a phone call to someone who is important to you.

20. Help a friend or sibling with their homework or a chore around the house.

Empathy

Empathy is seeing with the eyes of another, listening with the ears of another and feeling with the heart of another.
— Alfred Adler

Understanding and feeling another person's experiences and emotions is the practice of empathy. It is also defined as an appreciation for another's situation or point of view. It is important for us as parents to help children understand how another person may be feeling and what they are going through. Putting oneself in another's shoes can help to develop your child's sense of awareness as she differentiates her feelings from someone else's.

Things to Keep in Mind When Teaching Empathy

Most children have a natural affinity toward animals and others, but some do not. Research shows that when a child's emotional needs are met at home, they are better able to develop a sense of empathy.

It is important to model and practice empathy in our daily lives as much as possible. Pointing out injustices toward others or animals that call for empathy is a wonderful way to instill a natural empathetic response.

Be sure to focus on what your child has in common with others as well as what he doesn't have in common. Instill the understanding that it's okay to be different and to embrace our differences.

EMPATHY

ACTIVITY 1: Nature Walk

MATERIALS NEEDED

- a nature trail, park, playground, or any place nature can be seen

Taking your child on a nature walk allows her to express her spontaneous caring for living creatures. Take advantage of the teachable moments when a creature or beautiful plant is spotted. Encourage your child to be patient as she waits for a butterfly to land on her arm. How do we treat the butterfly when it lands? Should we pick the flower? Show them that the flower can be enjoyed just as much by leaning over and smelling it and looking at it closely while its roots are still in the earth.

Option: Children can use their gratitude journals to write or draw pictures of what they noticed on the walk and what they are grateful for.

EMPATHY

 Activity 2: Stand in My Shoes

MATERIALS NEEDED

none

Below are some scenarios to talk through with your child. After each, ask your child to imagine how that person must have felt, what he could do to help and how he would feel after helping someone in need.

- You are standing on the playground with several friends and you notice a boy being made fun of. You see the sadness on the boy's face, but the boy doesn't say anything as he is being teased. You have noticed that this boy comes to school in dirty clothes quite often. How do you show empathy?

- You come home from school and notice your mom sleeping on the couch. You are surprised because she is always waiting for you at the door. She tells you that she doesn't feel well. You remember what it's like to be sick. How do you show empathy toward your mom?

- You arrive at your friend's house and notice a big pot of flowers on the porch. The flowers look wilted and the dirt is very dry. You know your friend has many chores to do around the house because his parents work late. How can you help while showing empathy to both the plant and your friend?

EMPATHY

- It snowed for the first time last night and it's the perfect kind of snow for a snowman. You go outside to play and notice your elderly neighbor trying to shovel the heavy snow off of his steps. You really want to play in the snow. What do you do to show empathy toward your neighbor? How could you help? Could you still play in the perfect snow? Note: If your child is too young to shovel snow, point that out while asking for other suggestions of how they could help.

- You are on your way into school and you notice that a student has accidently dropped their backpack on the ground. Papers and books have spilled out and they are struggling to pick it up. You hear your friend calling you to catch up. What do you do?

EMPATHY

Activity 3: Toothpaste Challenge

MATERIALS NEEDED

- small tube of toothpaste
- small plate
- butter knife

Before beginning this activity, share an example of an experience in which you said something to someone you wish you hadn't. Ask your child if something like that has happened to him. Encourage him to share how he felt after saying something he regretted, and how he thinks the other person may have felt. Asking children to put themselves in another person's shoes is an important part of this empathy lesson. Then ask your child if someone ever said or did something to him that hurt his feelings. Again, how did he feel?

After you've talked, squeeze the entire tube of toothpaste onto the plate. Hand your child the plate and ask him to put the toothpaste back into the tube using the butter knife. Of course, your child will find that it's nearly impossible to get the toothpaste back into the tube! Explain that the toothpaste tube represents him, and the toothpaste on the plate represents unkind words or actions. Once we say or do something unkind, it's almost impossible to take it back. This is a powerful way to illustrate the importance of being mindful of how our words and actions can affect other people.

EMPATHY

ACTIVITY 4 — Family or Friend in Need

This is a good activity to do after practicing one or more of the previous empathy activities. Ask your child to quietly look for a friend or family member that may be in need. Perhaps a friend drops her papers as she gets on the bus, or a parent is doing multiple things at once in order to get dinner on the table. Or maybe someone is struggling to open a door. Encourage your child to respond and help out once he's noticed the need. Check in with him about how he felt while helping and how it might have made the other person feel when he offered to assist.

MATERIALS NEEDED

none

EMPATHY

Activity 5: Role Playing and Discussion

Activities that temporarily disable the senses or ability to move can help children understand empathy by personally experiencing a limitation someone else may be faced with. Below are two role-playing activities to bring awareness to the differences that others may be facing. Also included in this activity are conversation starters to help your child understand others who face physical and/or mental challenges.

Be sure to stay close to your child during this activity to make sure he is staying out of harm's way while his abilities are compromised.

ROLE PLAYING

Broken arm: Help your child use the athletic wrap or towel to wrap her arm against her body so she is unable to use it. Give her tasks to complete, such as carrying a basket, using technology, putting on a jacket or sweater or tying her shoes.

Being blind: Blindfold your child and have him navigate around a room to experience what being blind may be like. You can even give directions to enhance the experience.

MATERIALS NEEDED

- athletic wrap or towel

EMPATHY

After each role-playing session, you could ask your child these questions to create conversation about empathy:

- What difficulties or frustrations did you have during your experience?

- What could you do the next time you see someone with this difference?

- What would it be like to be a child who struggled with walking, talking, eating or playing?

- How would you feel if you had a similar obstacle?

Togetherness

If there ever comes a day when we can't be together, keep me in your heart, I'll stay there forever.
– Winnie the Pooh, A. A. Milne, The House at Pooh Corner

We all need our moments alone, to reconnect with ourselves and explore who we truly are as individuals. However, we also all need a sense of community. A sense of togetherness. Spending time with family, friends and neighbors can help form and solidify relationships, prevent loneliness and make us healthier. Studies have

shown that people who have a sense of community are happier and generally live longer than those who don't.

We can be part of another human being's life by sharing stories and celebrating accomplishments. We can take care of one another by showing empathy and compassion. A sense of belonging can help us feel safe and secure, knowing that we can lean on others for support and be there for those who need us to lean on. Cooperative games, like the first two activities in this section, are a great way to instill the importance of togetherness. These activities focus on teambuilding, cooperation and communication and are to be done with a larger group of people. Grab your friends and neighbors!

TOGETHERNESS

Activity 1: Circle Sit

MATERIALS NEEDED

- lots of friends or family members

The goal of this activity is to end up with each child sitting on the knees of the person behind her. Begin with everyone standing in a circle, arranging themselves so that there is another person of about the same size on either side. Everyone turns to the right. Have the group move a step or two closer to the center of the circle and place their hands on the waist of the person in front of them. Before they actually attempt to sit down, do a trial run to make sure everyone is standing close enough together. To do this, instruct everyone to bend their knees on the count of three, just touching their bottoms to the knees of the person behind them before standing back up. If everyone in the group does not touch the knees of the person behind them, readjust positions and try it again. Once each person is positioned correctly, instruct everyone to sit on the count of three. Tell them to concentrate on supporting the person in front of them, and trust that the person behind them will do the same for them. This is a great way to show teamwork and solidarity.

TOGETHERNESS

Activity 2: Pair/Group Sit

For this activity, children will work in pairs with someone of similar height and weight, standing back-to-back with arms linked at the elbows. From this position, the pair will attempt to sit down and stand back up without unlinking their arms. If they master this, combine children into groups of three or four. Build up to doing this with the entire group to encourage cooperation and patience.

MATERIALS NEEDED

- lots of friends or family members

Activity 3: Time at the Park or Playground

On a beautiful day, parks and playgrounds are usually full of people. Encourage your child to play with someone he doesn't normally spend time with. If he knows the idea is to play with someone new, it will make the idea more appealing and approachable. If you are in a park or other area where there are unfamiliar people, encourage your child to play with people with whom he's familiar, but doesn't usually play with.

MATERIALS NEEDED

- a beautiful day
- a park or playground

TOGETHERNESS

Activity 4: Treasure Hunt

MATERIALS NEEDED

- treasure hunt game designed by your child
- lots of friends or family members

Kids love treasure hunts! Spend an afternoon with your child creating a treasure hunt for someone else to play. Think up a theme then develop a series of clues or riddles that lead to a final prize. The sky is the limit here and nearly all spaces and places are great venues for a treasure hunt to take place. The general rules of a treasure hunt are:

1. Gather enough people to form teams of two or more.

2. All team members must stay together for the entire game.

3. If children are playing on teams without an adult, boundaries should be established for safety reasons.

4. Encourage children to be kind and respectful to those playing the game and those they may encounter while playing.

5. The goal of the treasure hunt is to work together to plan and play. Enjoy the game and congratulate the person or team who finds the final prize first.

TOGETHERNESS

ACTIVITY 5 Togetherness Time

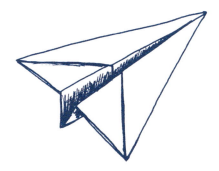

Plan a time each day or an evening each week to spend quality time together away from TV's, gaming systems and electronic devices. Use the time to play a card or board game, read a book, make paper airplanes or origami, cook a new recipe, wash the car or the dog, work in the garden, or assemble a jigsaw puzzle. Enjoy reconnecting with one another in this busy world we live in.

MATERIALS NEEDED

- puzzles, board and/or card games, Legos, books for shared reading, really anything that allows for time spent together

This book is dedicated to all of the beautiful families in the world. It is my hope that this book will provide you and those you love with the opportunity to spend time together, to make new connections and perhaps even reestablish lost ones. Most of all, I hope it gives you the chance to stop and notice those moments in your life that travel by so quickly. Life is a beautiful thing. Take time to pause and notice.

I would also like to express my gratitude toward my own beautiful family — may you always keep your beginner's mind.